I0199604

The Chancer

Reaching for Rock

Jayne Sbarboro

Copyright © 2025 by Jayne Sbarboro

When I'd landed in London three weeks earlier, I had my little tan thrift store Boy Scouts of America backpack. It was packed with clothes, gym shoes, rock climbing shoes and a vague idea that, if possible, I would climb. I had never imagined climbing a roof overhang in Chamonix, because I'd never heard of Chamonix. I had not imagined fourth-classing the Crib Goch Traverse in Wales either, but this is what comes of being a Chancer.

I learned this word talking to a Brit in a pub over a pint, so I looked it up. "A reckless, improvident, often somewhat unscrupulous opportunist." The word comes from British slang. I liked it—because except for the "unscrupulous" part, it fit me to a T. Being a Chancer had forced me to manage the fears that came from grasping at handholds and opportunities. Being a Chancer made me happy to be alive. As for the "improvident" part…well, I admit I did lack foresight.

I'd learned to rock climb in Southern Illinois, with its beautiful, deep forests of mossy cliffs and sandstone with fission pockets. There, I was a card-carrying member of the Shawnee Mountaineers. Hah! That very name was an oxymoron. The cliffs in the Shawnee forest don't reach higher than a bluff and often are less than a hundred feet high. No matter. We belayed each other on topropes and memorized by muscle the climbing sequence of overhanging rock faces.

There I had learned that Class I is an easy walk, across mostly even pathways. A nice ramble. Class II is a bit more of a hike with rolling terrain thrown in for fun, and Class III rolls up and down like a roller coaster. These rambles would hardly be in the category of "climbing," except they are part of the approach that gets you up to mountain terrain. Fourth-class climbing is scrambling—clambering up inclines that are steep enough to require using your hands to ascend, but not so steep that you think you will fall. If falling were a possibility, you would want a rope to protect you from falling very far. The Crib Goch Traverse on Snowdon turned out to be a fourth-class scramble, one where I sure would have taken a rope had it been offered.

In Southern Illinois, I had come to learn and love fifth-class rock climbing.

The Shawnee Mountaineers had carabiners and climbing ropes, courage, and camaraderie to spare. They taught me safety—always have three points of contact before testing a handhold for your next move. Don't use your knees, even if they are the most convenient thing to use. They're too hard to get off when you try to take the next step. When belaying, pull the rope into the belay device and use that same hand to slide the rope past the grip hand so that the grip hand never lets go of the rope.

It was a few years before I learned that fifth-class climbing came in two glorious flavors—toproping and lead climbing. In the late '70s and early '80s, sport climbing had not been invented. We toproped our climbs under the canopy of towering oaks and maples in Southern Illinois, warm sunlight coming through the trees in deep greens. Our sweat trickled in droplets and blended with the humidity. It was peaceful play in a woodland forest.

Toproping is like using a pulley, nylon webbing looped around a tree at the top with two carabiners on the loop to act as the pulley "wheel." Both ends of the rope dangle to the ground. One end is tied to the climber and the other end is gripped by the belayer. Toproping feels safer. If you fall off the rock face, you dangle close to the level where you came off. The belayer can hold you there while you have time to rest, to scrutinize the move you missed, reassess your stamina, or signal to them to lower you to the ground. And in Southern Illinois, toproping was the name of the game.

Fifth-class climbing feels like a dance. Weight changes, turns, arc of a reach, pivot of a foot, a chassé to the left necessitating a delicate balancing to the right. The rock face is a fascinating partner because every move up precipitates the need for a different problem-solving step. A graceful rock climber is an incredible athlete. On tough bouldering moves, we choreographed our movements to make our ascents.

I have read that in Gaelic, *anam cara* translates to "soul friend." I have never climbed in Ireland, but I lovingly think of rock as my sturdy anam cara. It is a friend I cradle while I admire its solidness and its ancientness. Touching, seeking, testing the rock's surface, my hand inches along carefully finding a niche, a handhold. Each finger notes how this niche, this hold, is exactly the place it wants to be. I fold my cupped hand around an edge, happy to rest with it. A really good handhold feels like a really good friend—it holds you up, gives you courage to reach for the next thing, and instills the confidence needed to keep going—the belief that when you get up to the next spot there will be another handhold in just the right place.

The dance of climbing is holding these rock curves and tenuous connections while moving your feet up, edging, crossing over in dance steps. Reach the highest place your foot can find to stick to—a little nub that the sticky rubber of your rock-climbing shoe grabs—and move upward. Because the rock is your dance partner. Explore each new potential handhold, admiring how geology created such a vertical trail for you to explore.

***

There I was, on a plane to London because a friend had talked me into taking a theater class with her in Chelsea College. It turned out that the director of the theater program sat right next to me on the flight. He was friendly.

"What will you do when you get there?"

And it hit me just then that I did not possess any kind of itinerary. I was going early to travel around, but I hadn't actually had the forethought to plan anything. I paused for a moment. My pack held my climbing shoes because I always carried them with me. I was a good rock climber. I knew I would do what I loved anywhere that I could. So I said, "I'm going to climb."

I said this confidently, making it sound like I had purpose—and pluck.

He nodded wisely, gracious enough not to laugh at the chucklehead sitting in the seat next to him. England, in truth, is not the first place you would go to rock climb. But it did happen to be the place where I was going, and that was the product of a different lack of planning.

In Victoria Station I queried, "Excuse me, can you tell me where I would go to climb?" I would have just asked but I was in England. I find it bloody strange that when I spoke to someone with a different accent, something made me think I should use their accent so they could understand me better. Brits hate this, but I couldn't help it.

The lady at the information desk was helpful.

"Well, if it's climbing y' want, I'd go to the Lake District," and she gave me clear directions.

Off I went, first by bus, to the English Lake District. I got off at Lake Windermere and climbed aboard a boat, the MV Swan, to take the lake cruise from Bowness to Ambleside. This antique merchant vessel from 1938 was outfitted with a tea and coffee bar in the mid cabin and—more important—a fully licensed bar downstairs. Lacquered wooden bench seating lined the decks. It was summer on one of the most beautiful lakes nestled in the fells of the English Lake District. This boat ride attracts locals as often as it does tourists to ride this beautiful ribbon of water. So I was immediately greeted by a crash of coworkers who were "on holiday" together. They were drinking to the day and everything in it and were already most of the way drunk.

"Where y' from, Darlin'?"

"Chicago ..."

Their glasses rose cheerfully, and they sang, "M-y-y-y kind of town, Chi-cahgo is!! My kind of town!" They bought me a beer, and I sang along. I only knew the chorus. They knew every word. It was grand.

The boat motored along the length of the lake, and I got off a few hours later. I'd met Peter on the boat, and it was getting late. Peter was a pleasant guy but not a romantic interest. If I were him, I would have just shaken my head. He could see a 22-year-old American girl, as clueless as the one he'd seen last week, explaining with a barely-believable story why she needed a place to stay. To make matters worse, she was talking in some form of American Brit-speak that barely made sense. Over pints, I explained my situation—or rather, my lack of planning.

Peter was ace. He offered me his barn, and I bought his meal because I didn't want to seem as cheap as chips. At that point in my trip, I still had money. Maybe that's when I first became a Chancer. Stateside, others might call me a plain old opportunist. After a pub dinner and with the help of this new friend, I slept under the hay wagon in his barn, in the deep countryside. And I was up, early as a squatter, to avoid being caught.

"Ta," I whispered in Brit-speak toward the house where Peter slept. Keeping calm, I practiced my "carry on." I walked briskly, looking left and right to remember the way.

Back in Ambleside, I found breakfast and the local bus to New Dungeon Ghyll. I arrived at the trailhead just before midday.

It was impossibly hot when I started up the trail to Pavey Ark. My jeans started to stick to my legs, making them chafe. My chambray shirt was soaked, as were the cloth straps on my canvas Boy Scout pack. Denim is not what you wear to hike or climb the fells of England. I wished I'd thought to change into shorts in the barn, but it had been cold then and I hadn't planned on this heat. Point in fact, I just hadn't planned at all.

I hiked … no, wait—I ambled up the steep path, amazed at just how grassy what they call *mountains* were. I couldn't see any sign of cliffs or rock faces, just a few gray limestone rocks that dotted the landscape. I stopped, discouraged, and sat on one. Along came a twenty-something couple. Wanting company, I casually asked, "Is this the way to climb?" I am as admired for my clever repartee as I am for my planning. They looked at my climbing shoes hanging outside my pack and considered the question.

"Well, if it's climbing y' want, then y' should go to Wales."

Wow.

All this way … and I was in the wrong country. They carried on. I realized I wasn't quite as calm as I'd felt earlier.

I sighed. I sat. Then sighed again and thought about it. The heat was draining. I was hungry, but I hadn't brought much food. Since I wasn't a master of preparedness, this didn't surprise me. It didn't bother me either. I scraped myself off the rock, deciding I should have at least a bit of a look.

I hiked up the Class 3 trail, more steep than rolling—and then, out of steam, I plunked down on a rock again. Up came another pair of Brits and I asked again, more to save myself effort and just in case I really was in the wrong place, "Is this the way to climb?"

"Em … yes."

I tried out my new language skills. "Mind if I walk it with you?"

"Shoor," they agree.

I got off my bum. My accent didn't fool them, but they were kind, and I yomped it up to the lake with them.

I learned that Pavey Ark is the largest cliff of the Langdale Pikes. It had truly sounded like the right place when I was in Victoria Station. Here, I found that its main face was an angled cliff, little more than a quarter mile across. Someone else might have been disappointed that such a tiny rock face was all there was, but not me. It was big enough to have rock climbers crawling all over it, and they looked like my sort of fun.

Stickle Tarn, the crystal lake at the base of Pavey Ark, reflected the blue sky in its clear beauty. I gazed at it longingly. It promised refreshment deep enough to be spiritual. And of course, I had not brought my suit. Not to worry. I'd brought my recent past with me—college days in local lakes where you wouldn't have worn anything to swim, even if you'd had the choice.

"Um," I said, with American nervousness. "Do you think anyone would mind if I didn't wear any clothes?"

"Em," she said with British calm. "I don't think so."

I frenzied off my clothes as fast as you could peel wet jeans and left them in a heap. I flowed into a lake that was as fully sweet and cool as it looked. Lazy strokes stretched my arms until I felt calm, happy, and worriless. No towel, of course, but it was easy to bask-dry in the sun. I hiked the remaining kilometer and rounded the tarn up to the climbers who were sorting their ropes at the base of Pavey Ark.

The climbers I've met have always been friendly types, and these were no exception. It wasn't hard to convince Chris, who had already set up his toprope, to let me climb with him. I wiggled into my dancing shoes—size eight EB rock-climbing shoes. These soft, rubber-soled canvas boots were popular in 1978 when I started climbing. And here, though they were four years old and wearing thin at the toe, they helped me prance up the 5.9 climb. I curled my fingers around escarpments and held hands with this ancient, weathered face. The concoction of air, sun, and place, laced with the view, was spiked. It was elixir enough to make me drunk on life. The people playing below in the lake and picnicking on its shores looked like they were having an equally fine time. The sky was cerulean. I soared.

Later, over a pint, Chris told me they were all proper members of the Fell and Rock Climbing Club of the English Lake District. I was impressed. I thought I recognized them as climbers, with the same sort of lure for adventure in their blood that flowed in mine. In any case, they offered me lodging in their club's hostel, which was a converted stone barn. We climbed again the next day, all short routes on this cliff face. It was glorious.

I know that there are higher and more rugged rock faces in other places in the world, but I learned that rock climbing as a sport actually originated in the Lake District. People never agree on one origin, though. Some say it started in the Dolomites; others say it was on the Elbe near Dresden. In any case, the most publicized first solo ascent was on the Napes Needle in England, in June 1886, and it inspired rock climbing as a sport. Napes Needle wasn't far from where I was.

And I was only about a hundred years late.

Over pints, they corrected my geography. THE place to climb is in WALES.

"Oh," I said.

And I thought, in a very proper British accent, *Feck*.

Llanberis, to be precise. Moreover, he told me the English climbers hung out at Pete's Eats. Chris was encouraging, "sartin"

I could pick up a climbing partner "theere." I don't know where his accent originated, but I wanted to speak his language. I dreamed in it instead.

Two weekends later, I set off for Llanberis.

***

Snowdon is a compact part of a bigger mountain range and contains four summits that are the highest peaks in the British Isles outside of Scotland. Yr Wyddfa is the highest.

This beautiful country held its own in a rocky, hardscrabble way. Off the bus, I stopped in at Pete's Eats, and true to advice, found John who was willing to have a climbing partner the next day. The climb he had in mind was the Snowden Horseshoe, a circular ten-mile route that Britons call a scramble. My climbing shoes went back into my pack for another day.

We started at Pen-y-Pas, our backpacks full of food and water. John was easy company. He told me he didn't rock climb, that he was a fell walker instead. He had ambled trails on rolling fells in Scotland and the Pennine Mountains, which are the backbone of the English Lake District. While I wouldn't be rock climbing on this adventure with John, I'd have the opportunity to see the view from the highest mountain in Wales, 1,085 meters (3,559 feet). The route summited four peaks. It was an opportunity I wanted. We shared snacks and stories of hikes and climbs as we ambled along. He shared his Kendal Mint

Cake, assuring me that it was what all mountaineers ate on climbs for quick energy. It was pure white sugar.

We made the shoulder of the horseshoe, a knob of mountain named Crib Goch, by ten in the morning. I never once pronounced this name right during the trek. It should sound something like *creep gōkh*. *Adventure* was much easier for me to pronounce, but *creep* was more what I did as we traversed the Crib Goch, a serrated arête that leads to the summit of Garnedd Ugain (1,065 meters), the second-highest peak after Yr Wyddfa.

The Crib Goch was a rocky fourth-class scramble. The clouds were intermittent, and there was a lake far below. I could see white nicks in the gray rock that I was holding onto for dear life, nicks that had been left by people hiking this same route in crampons. Wishing for a fixed rope, I humbly crept and scrambled along. The drop-off on both sides of the ridge intimidated me.

My senses were alert, hyperstimulated by fear. I fumbled across the ridge, hands grasping for handholds.

I remember my brother-in-law explaining the main difference in our perspectives. He was terrified of heights. When he watched his son scamper near the edge of a bluff, he panic-screamed, "ERIC!! GET OVER HERE!"

And I said, "Jeez! Take it easy!"

He said, "No, Jayne. You don't understand—where you see up, I see down! Where you see air, I see gravity!"

I was not blind to gravity, but I was developing a theory that fear is something you really have to learn to control—especially if you're going to be a Chancer. Learning to control fear is a life lesson that takes practice. There is no end to the lessons and

no end to the practice, as far as I can tell. On the Crib Goch traverse, I got to practice a lot.

We stopped not far across this traverse to eat lunch with a view. Perched on the ridge, we watched clouds gather in the valley to our right, then scale the slope as they moved toward us. The weather turned gray. The clouds rose cumulo-nimbly up to blanket us before tumbling over the knife's edge into the valley to our left. We literally had our heads in the clouds, and it was much wetter than I ever imagined, but I was happy to be there. After crossing the flatter terrain of Garnedd Ugain, we continued on in mist that turned to raindrops that turned to downpour. We made it to the top in a torrent.

In the little summit building, we gripped our coffee cups to loosen the edge of cold and numb. We watched in awe as the rolling clouds and rain eclipsed the last bit of mountain. The storm poured over the landscape. We didn't stay long at the summit because the view was obscured. Wrapping our wet things tighter around us, we started toward Y Lliwedd ridge, the twin-peaked mountain of 898 meters that completed the four-peak set, and it was downhill from there. When we got to John's car, we drove to a pub packed with locals. The storm had knocked out all the power in the valley. And when in doubt, drink! I had no problem tippling in this language.

"The Bar Nash," I repeated.

"Yes. In Chamonix," John emphasized. "Bar Nationale is where the English climbers hang out."

"France??"

"Absolutely!" He waxed enthusiastic on le Aguille du Midi, the nordwand, the Grand Jorasses, and other fantastic climbs. *Nordwand?!* I thought. I'd only read about it. *I could actually get to see it?* My excitement grew, until I realized that once again I was kind of in the wrong country. *Merde.*

***

I listened to the *krluck-krluck* of cogs as they caught their sprocket, held the ascent till the next cog caught, *krluck*. We clattered up the steep grade on the regional cog rail—the final 40-minute leg toward Chamonix and the base of the Mont Blanc massif, a mountain range in the Alps.

The straw-haired German with his huge rucksack talked to friends on the train. Two climbing ropes were cinch-smashed under straps, crampons visible near the over-flap, ice axes for self-arrest held securely to the compact sides.

I thought about my puny rock-climbing shoes in my little brown canvas Boy Scout pack. I brooded over my brand-new recognition that rock climbing was but one subset of alpining— along with ice climbing, hiking, and bleeding. Alpining was something I hadn't even known how to dream about until this train trip. And I guess if I weren't a Chancer, I still wouldn't know about it.

The German talked to friends with similarly huge haversacks, and I could only think how much sinew and effort it must take to heft a pack like that onto one's back, let alone carry it up an alpine route. I thought they must have been alpining their whole lives; they looked hopelessly intrepid and mature at twenty-five. Here were men who climbed mountains for easy sport and abseiled—the British word for *rappelled*—for fun.

"Mehrere gluggle Felsenteil der Traverse."

When I overheard "traverse," my ears perked up. I'd had to traverse, or cross to the next maneuver, on many climbs. The Crib Goch traverse in Wales had been an awe-inspiring gambit of a traverse. I eavesdropped, looking for an entrée into their conversation. I practiced my German in my head, but *shpay kenzee climbing Deutch*?" was about all that my usually talkative internal voices uttered.

"Es machte uns viel Mühe. Es geht immer so weiter." Hmmm. No translation.

"Aber die Aussicht war grossartig," rejoined his companion. "Und ab und zu die Nordwand."

Nordwand. My excitement grew. Stateside, *nordwand* meant "north face." My brain furiously sent guttural sounds to my mouth that were nowhere near Germanic. I casually covered my mouth to prevent the accidental spillage of whatever German pig Latin might sound like ... *oytsch-day attin-lay*?

They earned my reverence just sitting there, looking beautifully rugged and talking.

"Es ist eine schwierige route. Gluh-gluck-gluck Traverse des Grandes Jorasses glugga-gluck Rocheford arête glugga-gluck den Jorasses ..."

That's it! I thought. *I know I heard him say, "Grand Jorasses," and I distinctly overheard "Rocheford Arete."* Rocheford Arete is a difficult crossing on the Grand Jorasses route.

I couldn't begin to figure out what "glugga-gluck" meant.

I climbed off the train at its terminal in Chamonix. The streets were wet with rain, but the sun had come out to dry them. I asked, "Oo-ay-lay 'Bar Nash'?" in my best French, which I do not speak. I had been rehearsing this since Llanberis.

***

When I'd landed in London those several weeks back, I never imagined I'd be here in Chamonix. This is what comes from managing fear and seizing opportunities. This is what comes of being a Chancer.

I'd never come within a mossy inch of sixth-class climbing because it is the sort of mountain assault you attempt only when other classes are not an option. I've only read about it. Sixth class is done completely on the rope, using the rope as both protection and handhold. It's often called *aid climbing.* Class 6 climbing was the method of choice for the alpinists I met in Chamonix. They consider it very stable. Very solid. I considered it very frightening. For one thing, they like that the rope is fixed in place.

Unlike fifth class, or free climbing, the climber doesn't use handholds on rock faces, because they are too small or nonexistent. The climb is done with the aid of pitons hammered into cracks, fixed as high over head as possible. They click a carabiner into the affixed gear, and then clip rope to the carabiner. Jumars are ratcheting clamps that hold a dangling webbed ladder, or etriers. They are shoved up the rope one hand at a time, and the ratchet keeps them from backsliding.

Similarly, the climber doesn't use footholds, because they're either too small or nonexistent. Instead, they step up their webbed ladder to gain height. They affix their next higher protection point, clip in a carabiner, then shove-shove, step-step, they move up to place another piece of armor in the rock. A climber pushes and shoves, ratcheting higher and higher up the rock face. More an assault than a dance, jumaring is brute-force climbing, perfect for very strong men like the Germans I'd met.

***

I walked through wet streets and found my way to Bar Nash. Three British chaps sat at a round wire table on the patio. A chapeau was pushed low over one's eyes, and he asked the other guy for a fag, lighting the cigarette with hands cupped. Brown hair and brown eyes, another scanned the street and walkers. The third protected an empty coffee cup with ragged hands wrapped around it. They sat there, wiry Chancers, wondering what I brought their way. I'm sure that they schemed how to best work this foreigner. Maybe it was risky, but as a woman climber who had dangled with my life on an 11 millimeter line, I trusted other climbers. So I ventured, "Do any of you know where I could find someone to climb with?"

I could see they were English, so I said this in my bloody best, worst British accent.

They looked up. Sized me up and down. Thought they might make some money.

"Forty pounds and you pay pherique rides," said the chapeau. "I'll take you up."

I scratched my head. I heard "freak rides" before my brain translated it into *telepherique rides*—a gondola ride or ski lift—that would make climbing much easier and save on effort. I hadn't thought of that. These guys were talking alpining like it was a casual third language … and I only spoke rock climbing. They were cool, owning the fresh mountain air. But, just fresh from England, I practiced chancing.

"I only have four pounds." This was true.

The chapeau guy squinted, looked me up and down. He gave up and shrugged. "You can stay in our tent."

The other added, "We nicked a 20 kilo bag of potahtoes from the 'otel. You can 'ave some of those, if ye want."

"There's a free campground up across the river."

I drank water and listened to them talk about possible routes. The Grand Jorasses sounded grander—and closer—than ever. I ended up staying with them for three days. It turned out that they didn't own the air. In fact, they possessed the same grubbiness as climbers in Carbondale—wool socks worn too many days in a row and sleeping bags smeared with sweat from each day's climbing. Like me, they clutched nervous optimism each time they surveyed the possibilities of the next climb. These were my meager possessions as well.

Climbing is a game of tension, and they let me play. Tension is what makes ascent possible. Rope tension and muscle tension, climbing is a geometry of muscle, dexterity, grace, and gravity. My EB climbing shoes' rubber soles wrapped, soft as gum, around the curves of the granite. My weight made them stick. I gingerly crept my feet higher. My hands were damp, a thin smear of perspiration mixed with oil threatened to make me slip. I dipped my hand into the chalk bag that hung from my harness behind me, rubbed dryness, squinted into the sun and surveyed my possible moves. It didn't matter that we didn't top out with our heads in the clouds here.

They practiced sixth-class climbing, honing technique, hammering in pitons, and climbing etriers made of webbing to scale overhangs. I, unversed in such equipment, skipped using the etriers they'd left for me on the overhang. I climbed the route in the fifth-class language I knew best. I'd seen white chalk on handholds left by other climbers, and I followed the dotted line. I was happy dancing on rock faces. I cleaned the route as I went, grabbed the etriers and delivered them. They were surprised that I hadn't used them to ascend the short roof, but I hadn't needed them.

As we lay in the tent, helicopters droned incessantly over our heads. Listening to these guys, who had become fast friends, I put together that the unusual heat had caused unprecedented rock fall, which led to more deaths on the mountain. The Flight for Life helicopters were completely unnerving to my novice ears. I hadn't packed for alpining, since I hadn't known what I was doing when I left the states. These guys tried to help, suggested I could borrow their wool socks, an extra ice axe. They even loaned me some courage to fuel my dream. But in the end, I didn't have enough to make a go of it and was satisfied with climbing short routes with them. I didn't dare chance the Grand Jorasses after all.

I left with a first-class mountaineering dream firmly planted in me, one that fueled my move to Colorado. Being a professional Chancer has stood me in good stead. I don't take advantage of people, but I take advantage of every opportunity that shows its unpredictable face. I could wish I had better planning capabilities, but every single adventure has been worth the misstep.

My brother-in-law would probably tell me it's a thin line between bravery and stupidity. I'd have to agree. Traveling these distances between up and down, between air and gravity, I hope I always see up. I've had lots of opportunities to practice controlling my fears. Breathing helps me carry on when I may not be properly calm. It's all I've got. And when it comes to the line between bravery and stupidity, all I can do is mind the gap.

…AND OTHER CHANCES
in order of favorite managed fears and grasped opportunities

1. Via Ferrata, Via Delle Bochetta Centrale circling Cima Brenta (Tower of the Brenta), constructed in 1936 in the Italian Dolomite Mountains. Estimated fourth class, completed in 2015.

2. Pingora, northeast face; one of the pinnacles that form Cirque of the Towers, Popo Agie Wilderness in the Wind River Range, Wyoming. Fifty Classic Climbs of North America. Fifth class climb, 5.8, completed in 1985.

3. Via Ferrata, Whistler Mountain, in Whistler, Canada. Fifth class, estimated 5.5 in difficulty, completed in 2024.

4. Glacier Point up to Sentinal Dome, Yosemite National Park. California Glacier Point Road was closed, so this hike went from the valley floor to the summit of Sentinal Dome. There were only four people at Glacier Point that time. Estimated Class 2 difficulty (just long); completed in 2023.

5. Chief Stawamus Peaks 1, 2 and 3, Squamish, British Columbia, Canada. Fourth-class scramble with via ferrata sections. Completed in 2024.

6. Angel's Landing, Zion National Park. Fourth class, should be a via ferrata but instead requires climbing chains to complete it. Done in 2019.

7. Kendall Katwalk section of the Pacific Crest Trail, Snoqualmie Pass, Washington. Basically a Class 3 rolling backpack; completed in 2024.

8. Devil's Causeway, Flat Tops Wilderness, Colorado, fourth-class scramble, completed in 2025.

9. South Kaibab Trail to Phantom Ranch, out Bright Angel. Grand Canyon National Park, Arizona. Class 3 hike completed in 2010.

10. The Petit Grepon, south face. Rocky Mountain National Park, Colorado. Fifty Classic Climbs of North America. Fifth-class climb, 5.8, in 1985.

ABOUT THE AUTHOR

Jayne Sbarboro is the author of two books for children, *The Truest Heart: A Story to Share to Overcome Bullying* and *Bravest Hearts: Empowering Our Friends*. She lives and climbs in Colorado.